Treasures

A Reading/Language Arts Program

Mc Graw Hill **Macmillan McGraw-Hill**

Contributors

Time Magazine, Accelerated Reader

learning through listening

Students with print disabilities may be eligible to obtain an accessible, audio version of the pupil edition of this textbook. Please call Recording for the Blind & Dyslexic at 1-800-221-4792 for complete information.

A

The McGraw·Hill Companies

Macmillan McGraw-Hill

Published by Macmillan/McGraw-Hill, of McGraw-Hill Education, a division of The McGraw-Hill Companies, Inc., Two Penn Plaza, New York, New York 10121.

Printed in the United States of America

ISBN-13: 978-0-02-198808-2/1, Bk. 5
ISBN-10: 0-02-198808-0/1, Bk. 5
2 3 4 5 6 7 8 9 (027/043) 11 10 09 08 07

Treasures

A Reading/Language Arts Program

Program Authors

Donald R. Bear
Janice A. Dole
Jana Echevarria
Jan E. Hasbrouck
Scott G. Paris
Timothy Shanahan
Josefina V. Tinajero

Macmillan
McGraw-Hill

Unit 5 Adventures All Around

THEME: Express Yourself

THEME: Watch It Go

THEME: Inventions

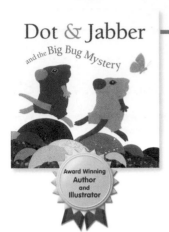

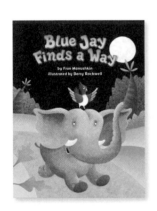

Talk About It

What kind of art do you like to make? How do you make it?

LOG ON Find out more about expressing yourself at **www.macmillanmh.com**

Express yourself

Words to Know

always
mother
father
try
firm
supposed
love

———

Jo**an**
bo**th**

 Read to Find Out

How is Joan's bedtime like your bedtime?

We Love Joan

Joan **always** stays up late. She likes to sing songs that she makes up. Her **mother** and **father try** to get her to sleep.

"We must be **firm** with her," they both say. "She is **supposed** to go to bed."

"Joan," says Mother, "No more songs. You must go to bed."

"We **love** you," say Mother and Father.

"I love you too," sings Joan.

Then she went to sleep.

Comprehension

Genre

A Fantasy is a made-up story that could not really happen.

Visualize

Fantasy and Reality

As you read, use your **Fantasy and Reality Chart**.

What Happens	Why It Could Not Happen In Real Life
1	1
2	2
3	3

Read to Find Out

What kind of pig is Olivia?

12

OLIVIA

written and illustrated by Ian Falconer

This is Olivia.
She is good at lots of things.

She is *very* good at wearing people out.

She even wears herself out.

Olivia has a little brother named Ian.
He's **always** copying.

Sometimes Ian just won't leave her alone,
so Olivia has to be **firm**.

Olivia lives with her **mother**, her **father**, her brother, her dog, Perry,

and Edwin, the cat.

In the morning, after she gets up,
and moves the cat,

and brushes her teeth,
and combs her ears,

and moves the cat,

 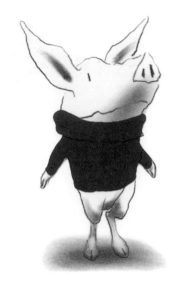 

Olivia gets dressed.

She has to **try** on everything.

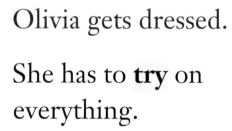  

20

On sunny days, Olivia likes to go to the beach.

She feels it's important
to come prepared.

Last summer when Olivia was little, her
mother showed her how to make sand castles.

She got pretty good.

Sometimes Olivia
likes to bask in
the sun.

When her mother sees that she's had
enough, they go home.

Every day Olivia is **supposed** to take a nap.

"It's time for your you-know-what,"
her mother says.

Of course Olivia's not at all sleepy.

On rainy days, Olivia likes to go to the museum.

She heads straight for her favorite picture.

Olivia looks at it for a long time.

What could she be thinking?

But there is one painting Olivia just doesn't get.

"I could do that in about five minutes," she says to her mother.

As soon as she gets home, she gives it a try.

Time out.

After a nice bath, and a nice dinner, it's time for bed.

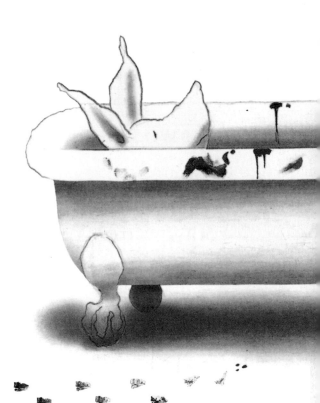

But of course Olivia's not at all sleepy.

"Only five books tonight, Mommy," she says.

"No, Olivia, just one."

"How about four?"

"Two."

"Three."

"Oh, all right, three.
But that's *it*!"

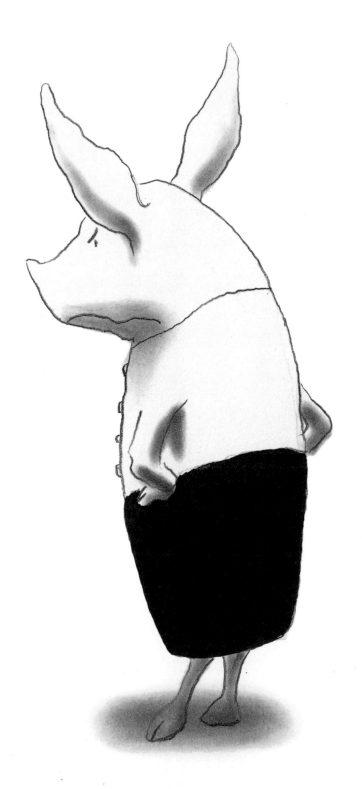

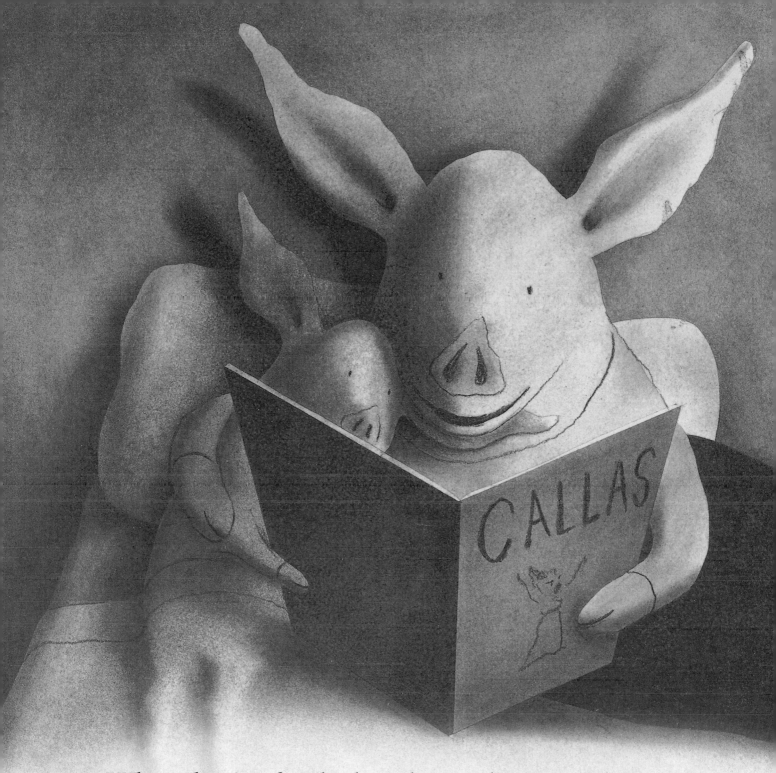

When they've finished reading, Olivia's mother gives her a kiss and says, "You know, you really wear me out. But I **love** you anyway."

And Olivia gives her a kiss back and says, "I love you anyway too."

Meet Ian Falconer

Ian Falconer says the characters in his book are based on his sister's family. His niece, Olivia, is very busy and wears out her parents, just as Olivia in the story does. He decided to make Olivia a pig because he thinks pigs are very smart animals and that they're like humans in many ways.

 Find out more about Ian Falconer at **www.macmillanmh.com**

Other books by Ian Falconer

Author's Purpose

Ian Falconer wanted to write about a smart pig. Write about another smart animal. Tell why you think it's smart.

Comprehension Check

Retell the Story

Use the Retelling Cards to retell the story.

Retelling Cards

Think and Compare

1. Could this story happen in real life? Why or why not?

What Happens	Why It Could Not Happen In Real Life
1	1
2	2
3	3

2. Do you ever act like Olivia? In what way?

3. Olivia likes to do creative things. What creative things do you like to do?

4. How are Olivia and Joan in "We Love Joan" alike?

Cats in Art

Fine Arts

Genre
Nonfiction tells about real people and things.

Text Feature
A Caption gives information about a picture.

Content Words
artists
colors
sculpture

 Find out more about art at **www.macmillanmh.com**

Cats, cats, cats! Look at all the ways **artists** have shown cats.

This painting shows a cat at home. The artist used a lot of **colors** and shapes.

Orange Cat on Couch was painted by Malcah Zeldis. She taught herself how to paint.

What shape are the cat's ears?

What color is the cat?

Where else do you see that color?

This cat is not a painting. It's a **sculpture**. What shapes do you see? Why do you think this artist named this sculpture *The Rattle Cat*?

The Rattle Cat by Alexander Calder is made of metal.

This sculpture of a cat and her kitten is very old. It comes from Egypt. How is this cat different from *The Rattle Cat*?

Cat and Her Kitten is more than 2,000 years old!

Cat and Butterfly was painted with watercolors.

This cat was painted a long time ago. It comes from China. The cat is looking up. Can you see what it is looking at?

How would you show a cat? Make your own cat painting or sculpture!

Connect and Compare

Which cat in "Cats in Art" do you think would be Olivia's favorite? Why?

Adjectives

An **adjective** is a word that tells more about a person, place, or thing.

Write an Invitation

Adam wrote an invitation to his art show.

Please come to my Art Show. It is on Friday, May 5. The show is in the big room with the red rug.

by Adam

Your friend,
Adam

Your Turn

Pretend your school is having an art show.

Write an invitation to your friends.

Writer's Checklist

☑ Will my friends know that I want them to come?

☑ Did I use adjectives correctly?

☑ Does each special name begin with a capital letter?

Watch It Go

See the Ball Fly!

Little Cub is up at bat. His mom and dad are calling to him.

"You can do it, Little Cub!" they **shout**.

Little Cub swings the bat, but he misses the **ball**. He hears some **laughter** and puts his **head** down.

Perhaps I **should** not be at bat, he thinks. Then he says, "I'll just do my best."

On his next try, Little Cub hits the ball. He sees it fly over the **meadow**.

"I've **never** done that before!" he says as he runs to each base.

47

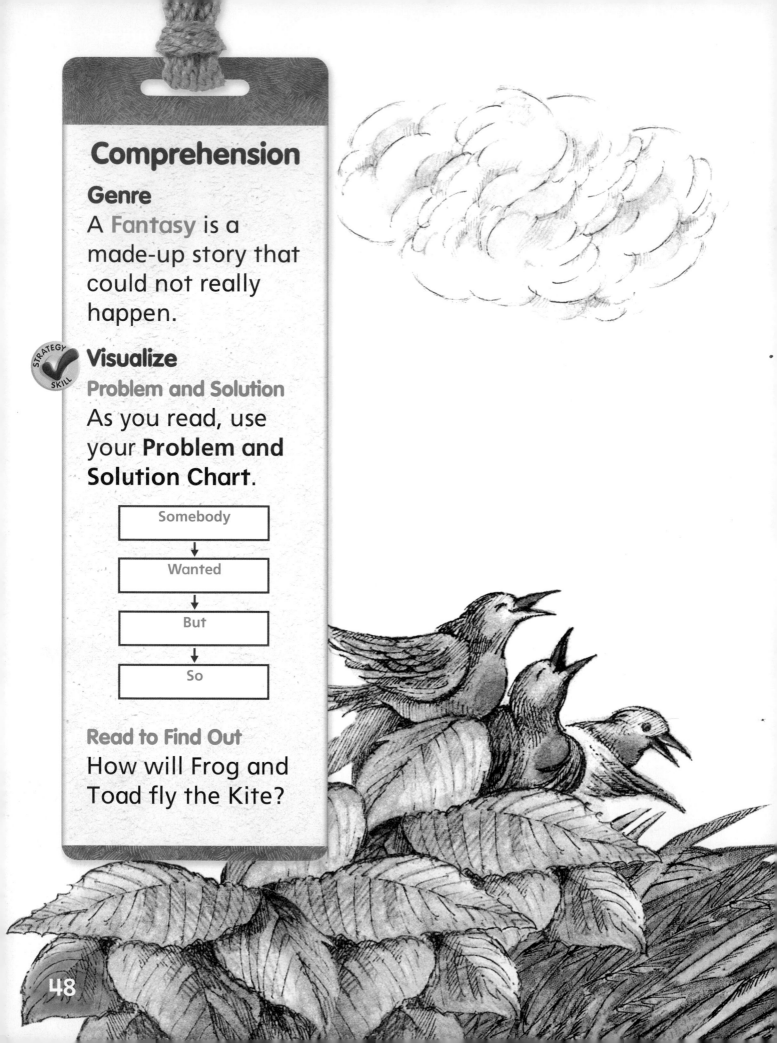

Comprehension

Genre
A **Fantasy** is a made-up story that could not really happen.

Visualize

STRATEGY SKILL

Problem and Solution
As you read, use your **Problem and Solution Chart**.

Somebody
↓
Wanted
↓
But
↓
So

Read to Find Out
How will Frog and Toad fly the Kite?

The Kite

from
Days with Frog and Toad

Award Winning
Author
and
Illustrator

by Arnold Lobel

Frog and Toad went out

to fly a kite.

They went to

a large **meadow**

where the wind was strong.

"Our kite will fly up and up,"

said Frog.

"It will fly all the way up

to the top of the sky."

"Toad," said Frog,

"I will hold the **ball** of string.

You hold the kite and run."

Toad ran across the meadow.

He ran as fast as his short legs

could carry him.

The kite went up in the air.

It fell to the ground with a bump.

Toad heard **laughter**.

Three robins were sitting in a bush.

"That kite will not fly,"

said the robins.

"You may as well give up."

Toad ran back to Frog.

"Frog," said Toad,

"this kite will not fly.

I give up."

"We must make a second try,"
said Frog.

"Wave the kite over your **head**.
Perhaps that will make it fly."

Toad ran back across the meadow.

He waved the kite over his head.

The kite went up in the air

and then fell down with a thud.

"What a joke!" said the robins.

"That kite will **never**

get off the ground."

Toad ran back to Frog.

"This kite is a joke," he said.

"It will never get off the ground."

"We have to make

a third try," said Frog.

"Wave the kite over your head

and jump up and down.

Perhaps that will make it fly."

Toad ran across
the meadow again.
He waved the kite
over his head.
He jumped up and down.
The kite went up in the air
and crashed down into the grass.
"That kite is junk,"
said the robins.
"Throw it away and go home."

Toad ran back to Frog.

"This kite is junk," he said.

"I think we **should**

 throw it away and go home."

"Toad," said Frog,

"we need one more try.

Wave the kite over your head.

Jump up and down

 and **shout** UP KITE UP."

Toad ran across the meadow.

He waved the kite over his head.

He jumped up and down.

He shouted, "UP KITE UP!"

The kite flew into the air.

It climbed higher and higher.

"We did it!" cried Toad.

"Yes," said Frog.

"If a running try

did not work,

and a running and waving try

did not work,

and a running, waving,

and jumping try

did not work,

I knew that

a running, waving, jumping,

and shouting try

just had to work."

The robins flew out of the bush.

But they could not fly

as high as the kite.

Frog and Toad sat

and watched their kite.

It seemed to be flying

way up at the top of the sky.

Arnold Lobel's Story

Arnold Lobel was often sick and missed many days of school when he was young. When he went back to school, he made friends by telling stories and drawing pictures. Many years later, Lobel's children liked to catch frogs and toads. Arnold Lobel loved the animals and wrote about them in his Frog and Toad stories.

Other books by Arnold Lobel

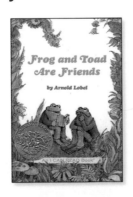

Find out more about Arnold Lobel at **www.macmillanmh.com**

Author's Purpose

Arnold Lobel wanted to write about good friends. Write about your friend. Tell how you help each other.

Comprehension Check

Retell the Story

Use the Retelling Cards to retell the story.

Retelling Cards

Think and Compare

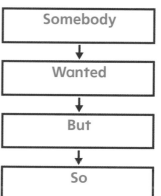

Somebody
↓
Wanted
↓
But
↓
So

1. What problem do Frog and Toad have? How do they solve it?

2. How do you feel when you try to do something hard? How does Toad feel?

3. How do Frog and Toad act like friends?

4. What do Little Cub in "See the Ball Fly!" and Frog and Toad have in common?

63

Toys That Fly

What toys can fly?

Balls can fly far and fast. Balls are round. Round is a great shape for throwing. How can you make a ball go where you want it to go?

Round **discs** can go far, too.
When you throw a disc, you
give it a spin. It spins like a
top as it flies. The spin helps it
to fly straight.

65

Toy planes can fly far and fast. Some toy planes don't need **motors**. They are called gliders. Wings help them **glide** on air. The tail helps steer the plane.

nose

wing

body

tail

Toy Glider

Kites don't look the same. But they are all made to glide on air. To fly, a kite has to catch the wind. Then the wind will push the kite up into the sky.

There are a lot of toys that fly! Which toys do you like to fly?

Connect and Compare

How would Frog and Toad try to fly a glider?

Adjectives that Compare

Add *-er* to adjectives to compare two.
Add *-est* to compare three or more.

Write About Not Giving Up

Lucy wrote about learning to do something hard.

My brother can go across the longest bars. I am smaller than my brother. I tried many, many times. My hands kept slipping. But then I did it!

Your Turn

Think about something that was hard to do.

How did you learn to do it?

Write about how you did not give up.

Writer's Checklist

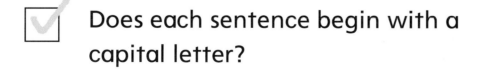

☑ Will the reader know how I feel?

☑ Do the adjectives that compare end with *-er* or *-est*?

☑ Does each sentence begin with a capital letter?

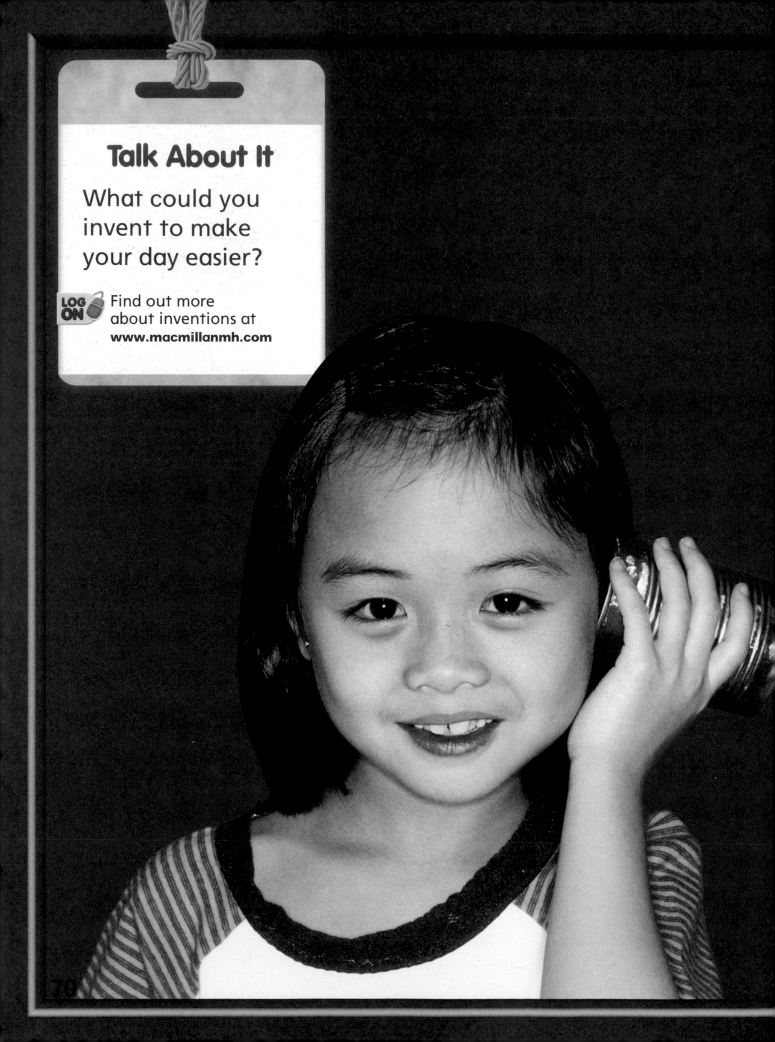

Talk About It

What could you invent to make your day easier?

LOG ON Find out more about inventions at **www.macmillanmh.com**

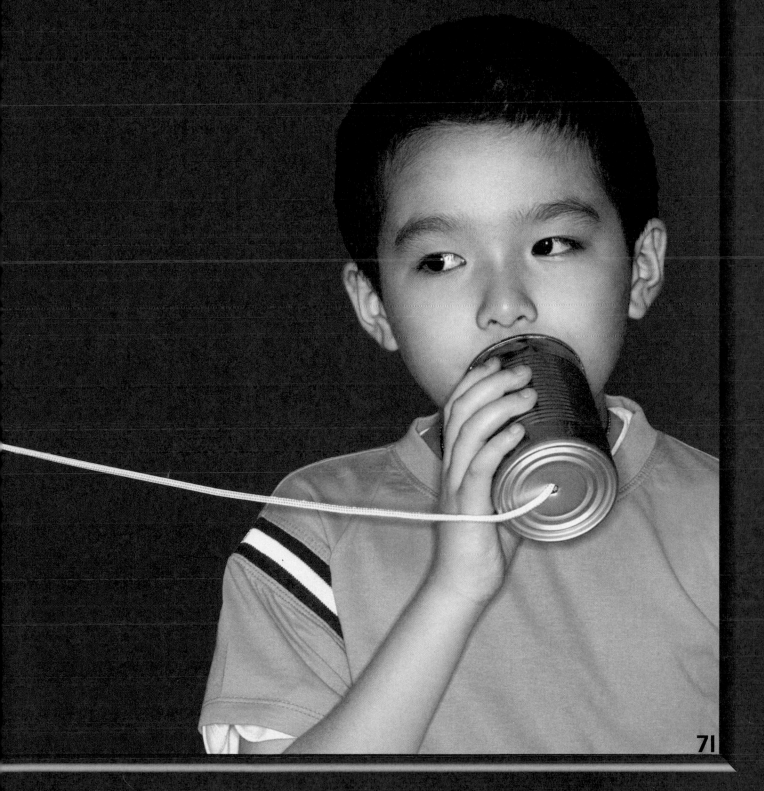

Inventions

Invent It!

Words to Know

children
round
better
machine
or
discovery

---

parts
start

You don't have to be big to invent things. **Children** can invent things, too. Look at the parts here. Could you make something with them? Where would you start? Where would the **round** parts go?

Where can you get ideas for things to invent? Think about things you need to do. Then think about how you could do them **better**. Is it hard to take your stuff to school? You could make a new kind of cart to help. You could make a new **machine or** game. You could make a great **discovery**!

73

Comprehension

Genre

A **Nonfiction Article** tells about real people and things.

Ask Questions

Cause and Effect

Why do the kids in this article invent things?

Jacob Dunnack

liked to stay at his grandmother's house. One day, he wanted to play baseball there. He packed his bat. But he forgot his baseballs!

74

Three balls fit
inside a "JD Batball."

Jacob asked a question. How could
he keep from forgetting again? He made
a **discovery**. There was a way to keep the
balls inside the bat.

Jacob drew a bat with a hole inside.
The **round** top came off. The balls fit
inside. That way, the balls would go where
the bat went.

Everyone liked Jacob's invention a lot!
His mother and father found a company to
make it. Now you can buy the "JD Batball"
in stores.

Shannon Crabill

always wanted to invent something. She thought about the clock that woke her up every day. She asked a question. What if you could pick the sound your alarm clock made?

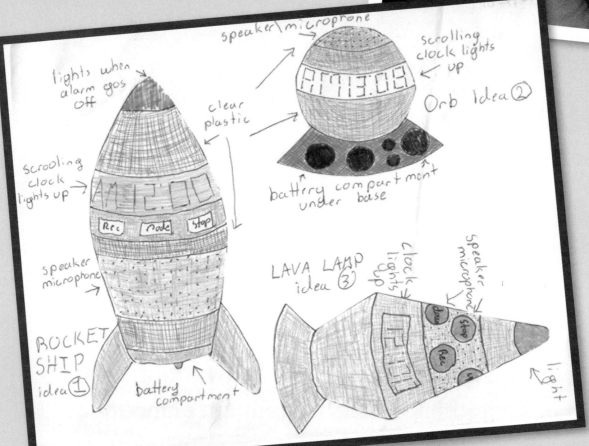

Shannon drew these ideas for her clock.

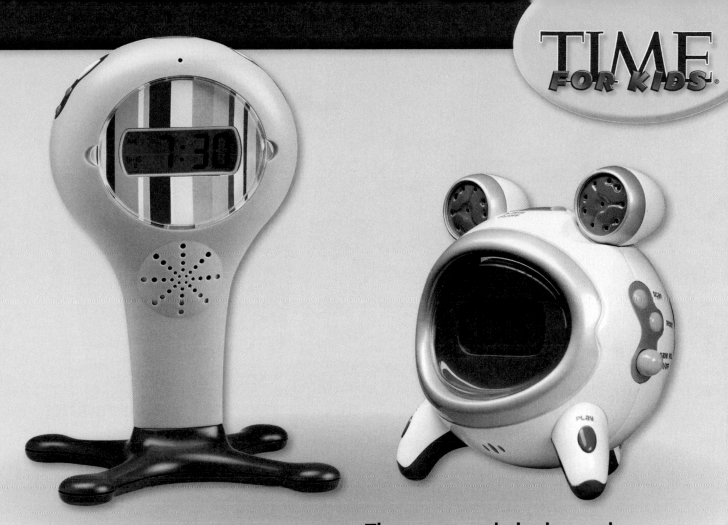

These are real clocks made from Shannon's ideas.

Shannon got an idea. You could record sounds on your clock. Then that sound could wake you up. The sound could be you talking **or** singing. It could be your dog barking or a song that you like.

Shannon sent her invention to a contest. She won the contest! Now, a company makes her clocks.

Spencer with his
brother and his mother

Spencer Whale's
invention helps sick kids.

When **Spencer Whale** was six years
old, he visited a hospital. He saw **children**
who had to take a big **machine** around
with them. The machine had medicine in
it. This made it hard for them to play.

Spencer asked a question. How could
he help these children play **better**? He had
a smart idea.

The children liked to ride in toy cars. But someone had to pull the medicine while they rode.

Spencer invented a part for the car that could hold the medicine. He drew his invention. People helped him make it. They put it onto the cars. Now sick children can ride and play with no help.

Spencer with his invention

Would you like to invent something, too? Would you like to invent a new toy? Or a machine that could help you? Try asking questions like these three kids did. Then see if you can find an answer!

Comprehension Check

Tell What You Learned

Describe how the kids turned their ideas into real things.

Think and Compare

1. What caused each of the kids in this article to invent something?

2. What would you like to invent? Why?

3. Think of an invention that helps people. Describe the invention and how it helps.

4. What might these three kid inventors want to make from the parts shown in "Invent It!"?

 **Test Strategy**

Author and Me
Think about what the author tells you. Think about what you know.

Helping Drivers See

Mary Anderson was an inventor. She lived about 100 years ago. Back then, when it rained or snowed, drivers had to get out of their cars to clean their windows.

Mary had a great idea. She invented a new way to clean car windows. It was a rubber blade that swung back and forth across the window. The blade scraped off water and snow.

This blade was the first windshield wiper. It worked like the wipers on cars do today. But it did not move by itself. Drivers made it move by turning a handle inside the car.

Go On ▶

Directions: Answer the questions.

1. What is this story MAINLY about?

○   ○   ○

2. Why did Mary invent the windshield wiper?

○ to help new drivers

○ to help wash cars

○ to help drivers see when it rained or snowed

Tip
Think about what you know.

3. How do wipers work today?

○ The driver gets out of the car to use them.

○ The wipers move by themselves.

○ Drivers turn a handle inside the car.

Write About an Invention

Alma thought of an invention that could carry her backpack. She wrote about how to make it.

How to Make a Backpack Cart
1. Get a skateboard and a box.
2. Tie the box to the skateboard.
3. Put your backpack in the box.
4. Tie a rope to the skateboard.
5. Now pull it.

Your Writing Prompt

Think of something you would like to invent. Draw a picture of your invention. Write directions that tell how to make it. Write down each step to take.

Writer's Checklist

☑ Are my steps easy to follow?

☑ Did I include details?

☑ Did I check my writing for mistakes?

Talk About It

What is something hard that you have learned to do? How did you learn?

LOG ON Find out more about doing new things at www.macmillanmh.com

I Can Do It

Words to Know

early

instead

thought

nothing

errand

suddenly

along

Cory

sport

Read to Find Out

How does Cory feel at the end of the story?

Nothing Stops Cory

Cory woke up very **early**. **Instead** of going back to sleep, she got out of bed. "I'm going to swim today," she **thought**. "**Nothing** can stop me."

Mom had to do an **errand**. Then she drove Cory to her swim class. **Suddenly**, Cory was in the water **along** with her teacher, Shelly.

Shelly held Cory's hands. Then she let go. Cory was swimming! "This is the best sport for me," she thought.

Comprehension

Genre
Realistic Fiction is a made-up story that could really happen.

Ask Questions
Make Inferences
As you read, use your **Inference Chart**.

Text Clues	What You Know	Inferences

Read to Find Out
How does Peter feel about learning to whistle?

90

Whistle for Willie

by Ezra Jack Keats

Award Winning
Author
and
Illustrator

Oh, how Peter wished he could whistle!

He saw a boy playing with his dog. Whenever the boy whistled, the dog ran straight to him.

Peter tried to whistle, but he couldn't.
So **instead** he began to turn himself around—
around and around he whirled . . .
faster and faster . . . .

When he stopped
everything turned
down . . .
and up . . .

and up . . .
and down . . .
and around
and around.

Peter saw his dog, Willie, coming.
Quick as a wink, he hid in an empty
carton lying on the sidewalk.

"Wouldn't it be funny if I whistled?" Peter **thought**.
"Willie would stop and look all around to see
who it was."

Peter tried again to whistle—but still he couldn't.
So Willie just walked on.

Peter got out of the carton
and started home.
On the way he took some
colored chalks out of his pocket
and drew a long, long line
right up to his door.

He stood there and tried to whistle again.
He blew till his cheeks were tired.
But **nothing** happened.

He went into his house and put on his father's old hat to make himself feel more grown-up. He looked into the mirror to practice whistling. Still no whistle!

When his mother saw what he was doing, Peter pretended that he was his father.

He said, "I've come home **early** today, dear. Is Peter here?"

His mother answered, "Why no, he's outside with Willie."

"Well, I'll go out and look for them," said Peter.

First he walked **along** a crack in the
sidewalk. Then he tried to run away
from his shadow.

He jumped off his shadow,
but when he landed they were
together again.

He came to the corner where the
carton was, and who should he
see but Willie!

Peter scrambled under the carton.
He blew and blew and blew.
Suddenly—out came a real whistle!

Willie stopped and looked around to see
who it was.

"It's me," Peter shouted, and stood up.
Willie raced straight to him.

Peter ran home to show his father and mother what he could do. They loved Peter's whistling. So did Willie.

Peter's mother asked him and Willie to go
on an **errand** to the grocery store.

He whistled all the way there,
and he whistled all the way home.

Getting to Know
Ezra Jack Keats

Ezra Jack Keats sold his first painting when he was eight years old! When he grew up, he created many books for children. He used cut-out paper and a special type of paste to make the bright pictures. He won many awards for his work, but was most pleased by letters from children who had read his books.

Other books
by Ezra Jack Keats

 Find out more about Ezra Jack Keats at **www.macmillanmh.com**

Author's Purpose

Ezra Jack Keats wanted to write about a boy who wished he could whistle. Write about something you wish you could do. Tell why you want to do it.

Comprehension Check

Retell the Story

Use the Retelling Cards
to retell the story.

Retelling Cards

Think and Compare

Text Clues	What You Know	Inferences

1. How do you think
   Peter feels about Willie?

2. Would you like to have
   Peter as your friend? Tell
   why or why not.

3. How is Willie a good pet?

4. What did Cory in "Nothing Stops
   Cory" and Peter both learn?

A Winning Swimmer

Kate Pavlacka can swim fast. She can run fast. She likes to read and write. Kate is blind.

Kate with her college swim team

Kate went blind when she was 14 years old. But that did not stop her. She swam on her school swim team. She became a very good **athlete**.

Water sprays Kate at the end of a lap.

Kate's coach helped. Kate couldn't see how to do a stroke. So her coach moved her arms and legs. That way she could feel how to do it. At the end of a lap, water sprayed her. That told her to swim the other way.

Kate dreamed of swimming in the Paralympics. These are games for athletes like Kate who have **disabilities**.

She swam and swam to get fit. And soon her dream came true. At the Paralympics, Kate swam very fast. She set **records**. Kate is a champ both in and out of the water.

Kate and her teammates

The Paralympics

Athletes with disabilities compete in the Paralympics. The games are held every four years. They began in 1960. There were only a few athletes and a few kinds of games back then. Now many athletes from all over the world come together to compete in many kinds of games.

Tennis and running are both Paralympic events.

This graph names some Paralympic games. It shows which games kids in a first grade class liked best. Which game do most kids like best? Which game do you like best? What about the kids in your class?

Favorite Paralympic Events

	soccer	running	swimming	basketball
8				
7	Daisy			
6	Anika			
5	Anna			
4	Lily			Alex
3	Kyra	Amir	Natalie	Stefan
2	Visay	Kate	Mike	Carlos
1	Molly	Joe	Sue	Manuel

Connect and Compare

How do Peter in *Whistle for Willie* and Kate Pavlacka both learn to do hard things?

Write a How-To

Writing

Number Words

Number words are adjectives that tell how many people, places, or things there are.

Ravi wrote about how to play a game.

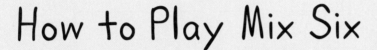

How to Play Mix Six

1. Write a sentence that has six words.

2. Cut the words apart and mix them up.

3. Tell your friend to put the sentence back together.

hid under box the Peter big

Your Turn

What new thing have you learned to do this year?

Write how to do it.

Writer's Checklist

☑ Are my directions clear?

☑ Are my sentences in the right order?

☑ Do I use number words correctly?

How Does It Grow?

Talk About It

How do plants grow?

LOG ON Find out more about plants at **www.macmillanmh.com**

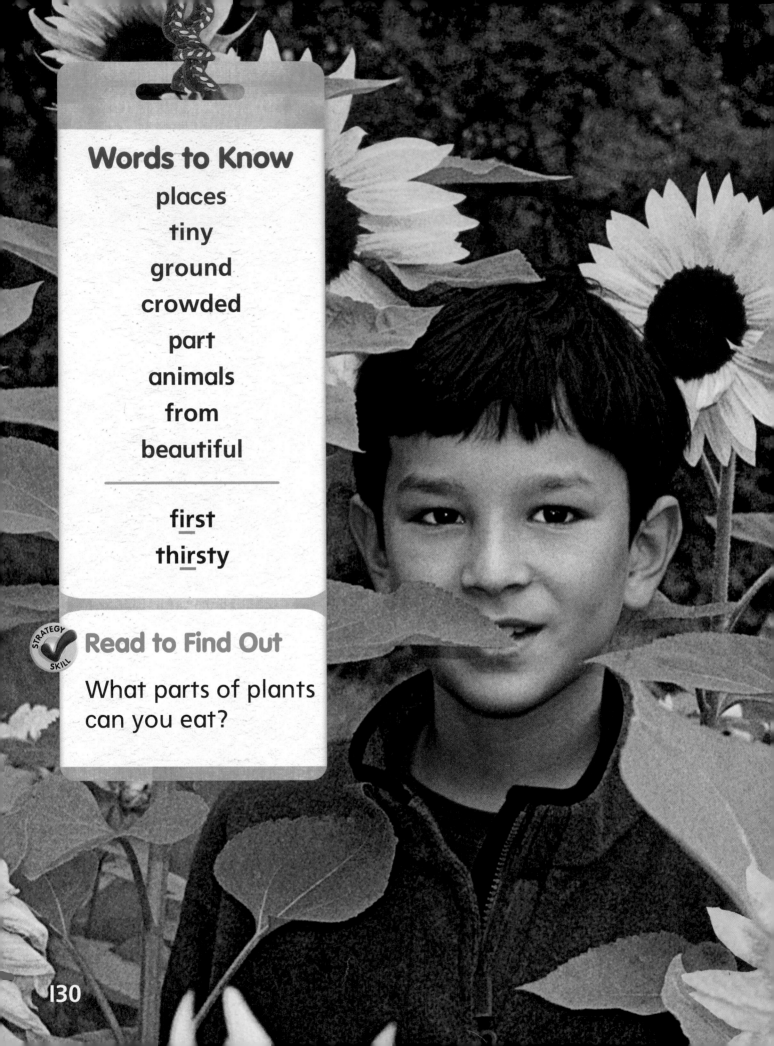

Words to Know

places

tiny

ground

crowded

part

animals

from

beautiful

---

f<u>ir</u>st

<u>th</u>irsty

Read to Find Out

What parts of plants can you eat?

STRATEGY SKILL

Beautiful Plants

Do you want to grow plants?

There are many **places** to plant. Find a place that is sunny. First, place the **tiny** seeds in the **ground**. Don't plant the seeds close together. They will be too **crowded** as they grow. Water them so they won't be thirsty.

We eat some plants. We eat the top **part** of peas, beans, and corn. We eat the part of yams and beets that grows under the ground.

If you are growing these plants, put up a gate. It will keep **animals from** getting them. They like to dig up your **beautiful** plants so they can munch on them!

Comprehension

Genre

Nonfiction gives information about a topic.

Ask Questions
Classify and Categorize
As you read, use your **Classify and Categorize Chart**.

One Seed	Many Seeds
1	1
2	2

Read to Find Out
What fruits have one seed? What fruits have many seeds?

A Fruit Is a Suitcase for Seeds

by Jean Richards
illustrated by Anca Hariton

Most plants have seeds. When you put a seed in the **ground** and water it, a new plant will grow **from** it. First, a seedling peeks out of the dirt. Then it grows into a plant.

Seeds often travel to faraway **places**.
If seeds did not travel, too many
plants would grow in one place. It
would be very **crowded**!

Some seeds travel on the wind.
Some seeds travel in the water.
Many seeds travel inside fruits.

pomegranate

The fruit is like a suitcase for the seeds.
It protects them on their trip.

Fruits look **beautiful** and taste good, so **animals** and people eat them, and drop the seeds in different places.

Some fruits carry one big seed
inside them. The seed is called a pit.
A cherry is one of these fruits.

peach

plum

apricot

Some fruits have many small
seeds inside them. An apple is
one of these fruits.

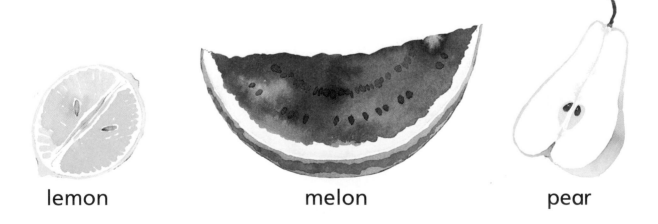

lemon   melon   pear

Some fruits have many, many **tiny** seeds inside them. A kiwi is one of these fruits.

blueberry

banana

Many berries, such as
strawberries and blackberries,
carry their seeds on the outside!
Raspberries do too.

Some vegetables we eat are really fruits. They carry seeds too. Peas are seeds.

tomato

butternut squash

Can you find the seeds on this ear of corn?

Hint: it's the **part** you eat.

I'll bet you didn't know that every
time you eat a peach, a cherry,
an avocado, a plum, a cucumber,
a tomato, a grape, an apple, an
orange, a pea, a pear, a melon, a
banana, or a blueberry,

you're really eating a suitcase...

...a suitcase for seeds!

Anca Hariton's
Colorful World

Anca Hariton started drawing with colored pencils when she was a child. She likes to write and draw pictures for books about the miracles of nature.

LOG ON Find out more about Anca Hariton at **www.macmillanmh.com**

Illustrator's Purpose

Anca Hariton wanted to draw things in nature. Draw a fruit you like. Tell what it looks like on the outside and what its seed looks like.

Comprehension Check

Retell the Story

Use the Retelling Cards to retell the story.

Retelling Cards

Think and Compare

1. Which fruits have one big seed? Which fruits have many smaller seeds?

One Seed	Many Seeds
1	1
2	2
3	3

2. Which fruits and vegetables in the story do you eat? Which do you like best?

3. How do seeds that travel help people and animals?

4. What do *A Fruit Is a Suitcase for Seeds* and "Beautiful Plants" each tell about plants?

Poetry

Genre
Poetry often describes the world around us in unexpected ways.

Literary Element
Many poems have a **Rhyming Pattern**. In some poems, the second line in a verse rhymes with the fourth line.

LOG ON Find out more about growing plants at **www.macmillanmh.com**

READ TOGETHER

Flowers at Night

by Aileen Fisher

Some flowers close their petals,
blue and red and bright,
and go to sleep all tucked away
inside themselves at night.

Some flowers leave their petals
like windows open wide
so they can watch the goings-on
of stars and things outside.

Connect and Compare

How is the author's purpose in *A Fruit Is a Suitcase for Seeds* different from this poet's purpose?

Writing

Antonym

An **antonym** is a word that means the opposite of another word.

Write a Poem About Fruit

Ruby wrote a poem about bananas.

I love bananas.
Some are big.
Some are little.
But they are all soft
and yellow.

Your Turn

Write a poem about a fruit you like.

Tell what it looks like, feels like, or tastes like.

Writer's Checklist

☑ Do I write details about my favorite fruit?

☑ Do I include describing words?

☑ Do I use synonyms or antonyms in my poem?

TEST PREP **Test Strategy**

Author and Me
Think about what the author tells you. Think about what you know.

All About Giraffes

What Can You See?

What can you see way up high,

With your neck reaching the sky?

Your feet look so small,

But your legs make you tall!

Go on ▶

The Tall Giraffe

Giraffes are the tallest mammals.
They have very long necks and legs.
A male giraffe is called a bull.
They can be as tall as 19 feet.
A female is called a cow.
They can be as tall as 16 feet.

A giraffe's long neck helps it eat leaves in trees. The leaves have water in them. So the giraffe can get a drink, too.

Go on ▶ 155

Tip

Think about what you know.

Directions:
Answer the questions.

I. How is the giraffe in the poem like other giraffes?

○ It needs a lot of water.

○ It has long legs.

○ It has spots like a cow.

2. Why do giraffes live near trees?

○ They like shade.

○ They don't like the sky.

○ They eat leaves.

3. Where does a giraffe get water?

○   ○   ○

Go on ▶

Writing Prompt

Write about your favorite wild animal.
Tell why you think it is the best animal.
Write four or more sentences.

STOP 157

Bugs, Bugs, Bugs!

Talk About It

What bugs do you know? What are they like?

LOG ON Find out more about bugs at **www.macmillanmh.com**

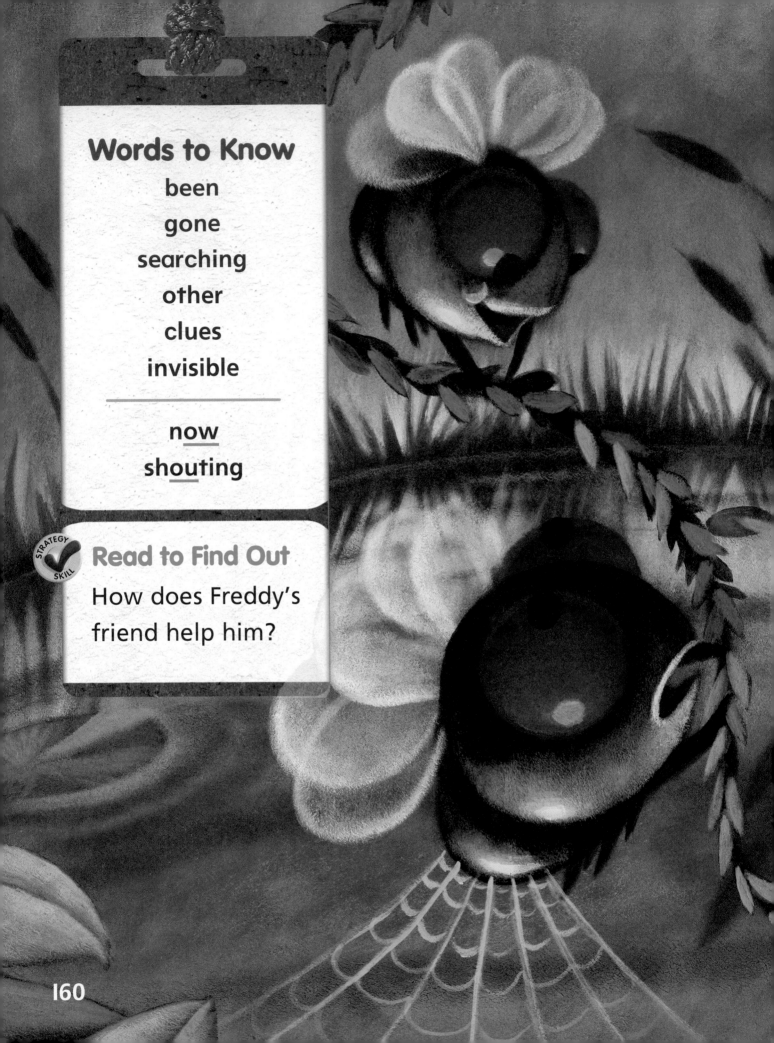

Words to Know

been
gone
searching
other
clues
invisible

_____

n<u>ow</u>
sh<u>ou</u>ting

STRATEGY SKILL

Read to Find Out

How does Freddy's
friend help him?

Where Has Freddy Gone Now?

Fern and Freddy have always **been** best friends. So Fern was sad when she couldn't find him.

"Where has he **gone**?" she said. "I must start **searching** for him now."

Fern went from one end of the pond to the **other**. But she couldn't find any **clues**.

"He's not **invisible**," she said.

Then Fern heard Freddy shouting. He was trapped in a web. In a flash, Fern pulled him out.

"Let's get out of here!" said Freddy, and off they went.

Comprehension

Genre

In a **Mystery**, the characters use clues to figure something out.

Reread

Use Illustrations

As you read, use your **Illustrations Chart**.

Illustration	What It Shows

Read to Find Out

Where do Dot and Jabber find bugs?

Dot and Jabber
and the Big Bug Mystery

by Ellen Stoll Walsh

Award Winning
Author
and
Illustrator

Dot and Jabber, the mouse detectives, were looking for a mystery to solve. They walked through the meadow and stopped to watch some bugs.

165

The mice thought they heard something. They turned to see, and when they turned back, the bugs had disappeared.

"Wow," said Jabber. "The bugs vanished. Poof!"

"They must be around here someplace," said Dot. "They couldn't have **gone** away so fast."

166

"Then they're **invisible**," said Jabber. "I can't see them at all, and I'm looking."

"Come on, Jabber," said Dot. "This is the mystery we've **been** looking for. Let's find those bugs! We need to look for **clues**."

"Dot, listen," Jabber whispered. "I think I hear one."

"One what?" said Dot.

"One clue. *Shhh*. Let's go check."

The mice crept over the hill.

"It's a sparrow," Jabber said. "No wonder the bugs disappeared. Sparrows eat bugs."

"Not me," the sparrow said. "I'm going to find some berries. They don't vanish when you want one."

And he hopped off.

"Now that the sparrow is gone," said Dot,
"why don't the bugs come back?"

"They're hiding from the toad," said a rabbit.
"Toads eat bugs, too."

"Where is the toad?" said Dot.

"Hiding from things that eat toads," said the rabbit.

"I don't get it," said Jabber. "Everybody's hiding, but I don't see anyplace to hide."

"Maybe we don't know how to look," said Dot. "Let's keep **searching**. The bugs can't be far away."

"They're watching us," said Jabber. "I can feel it."

"I can, too," said Dot.

"This gives me goose bumps," said Jabber. "They can see us, but we can't see them. I wonder what else is out there watching us?"

Dot caught her breath. "Jabber, quick. Something moved."

"I don't see it," said Jabber.

"Look," said Dot. "It's moving again."

Some butterflies rose from the meadow
and flew away.

"Wow, butterflies!" said Jabber. "I think the butterflies are a clue. They were hiding in plain sight, and we didn't even see them. Maybe the **other** bugs are hiding in plain sight, too."

"Oh!" said Dot. "Do you mean they're pretending to look like something else? Let's see if you're right."

"Dot," said Jabber. "Do rocks breathe?"

"Of course not," said Dot.

"Then I've found the toad."

"Jabber," said Dot. "I found the bugs!"

"*Shhh*," said a grasshopper.

"You're right, Dot. There are lots of bugs here!" said Jabber. "We just have to know how to look."

The grasshopper sighed. "Go ahead. Tell the toad where we are. Tell the whole world. What are a few bugs, more or less? I'm out of here."

"Wait for us!" said the other bugs.

"Well," said Dot, "the bugs have really disappeared now. But not before the great mouse detectives solved another mystery!" Dot looked around. "Jabber, where are you?"

"Try to find me," said Jabber. "I'm hiding in plain sight!"

Making Pictures with Ellen Stoll Walsh

Ellen Stoll Walsh says, "We have always loved stories in my family." When she started reading stories to her son, she decided to write and make pictures for children's stories, too. She often makes the animals in her books out of cut paper. She uses colored ink for her drawings.

Other books by Ellen Stoll Walsh

LOG ON — Find out more about Ellen Stoll Walsh at **www.macmillanmh.com**

Mouse Paint
Ellen Stoll Walsh

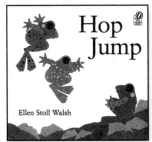

Hop Jump
Ellen Stoll Walsh

Author's Purpose

Ellen Stoll Walsh wanted to write a story about mice. Write about an animal you like. Tell about where it lives.

Comprehension Check

Retell the Story

Use the Retelling Cards to retell the story.

Retelling Cards

Think and Compare

Illustration	What It Shows

STRATEGY SKILL

1. How do the pictures help you understand the story?

2. What part of the story did you like best? Tell why.

3. Why do the bugs in the story seem to disappear? Have you seen other animals disappear like that?

4. How would Dot and Jabber look for Freddy in "Where Has Freddy Gone Now?"

The World of Insects

Insects are everywhere. There are more **insects** than any other kind of animal.

Kinds of Insects

There are all kinds of insects. The ladybug, housefly, and ant are all insects.

Some insects can fly. Many insects can not. Some live in water. But most live on the land. Some kinds of insects live and work together, like bees or ants. But most insects do not.

The Body of an Insect

All insects have six legs. All insects have three body parts. Insect bodies have no bones. The outside of an insect's body is hard. The hard outside **protects** its insides. Many insects have antennas.

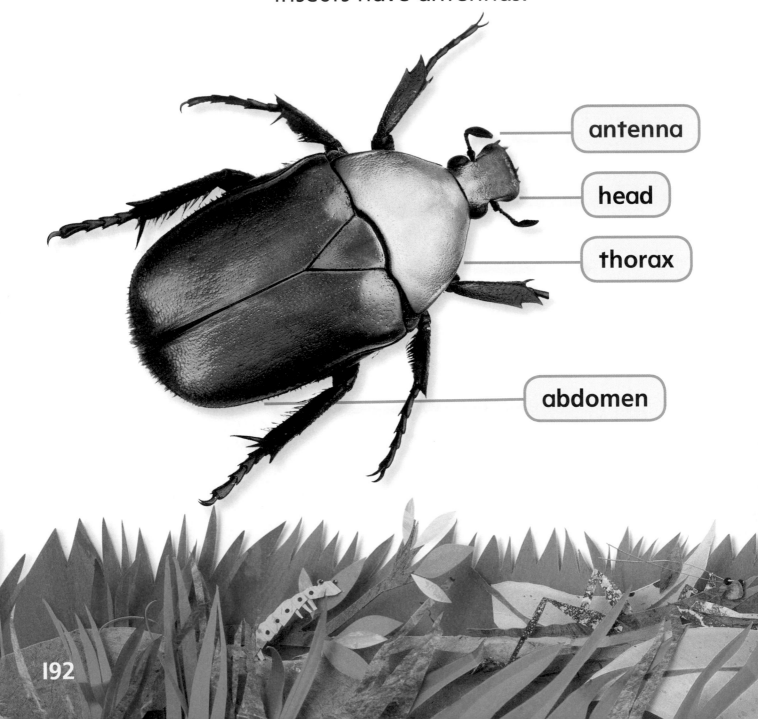

antenna

head

thorax

abdomen

Insect Senses

Insect **senses** are not like people's senses. Many insects smell with their antennas. Bees taste with their antennas. Flies taste with their feet.

Insects do not see the same as people do. Some insects have more than two eyes. A grasshopper has five eyes. It can see on all sides.

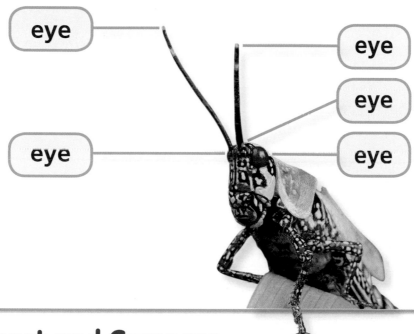

eye
eye
eye
eye
eye

Connect and Compare

How are the insects in *Dot and Jabber and the Big Bug Mystery* like the insects in this article?

Writing

Subjects

The **subject** of a sentence tells who or what the sentence is about.

Write About a Bug

Ryan wrote about a dragonfly that he saw.

I saw a dragonfly at the pond. It was a really big bug. Its wings were long and shiny. The dragonfly was very fast. I saw it catch a bee!

Your Turn

Think about a bug you have seen.

Tell what the bug looked like.

Tell what the bug did.

Writer's Checklist

☑ Do my sentences make sense when I read them aloud?

☑ Does each sentence have a subject?

☑ Does each sentence end with the correct mark?

Exploring Space

Talk About It

What do you think it is like to travel into space?

LOG ON Find out more about exploring space at **www.macmillanmh.com**

197

Words to Know

bear
helmet
birds
Earth
space
table
guess
fooling

g<u>oo</u>d
t<u>oo</u>k

Read to Find Out

Does Kim really go into space?

A Good Trip into Space

Kim curled up with her teddy **bear** and went to sleep. In her dream, she put on a red **helmet**. Then, she took off. She waved to the **birds**. She waved to **Earth** and began her trip into **space**. Soon she landed on Mars and walked over to a **table**. It was filled with good things to eat. So she sat down and had a great meal.

Kim's mom was waking her up. "Mom, you will never **guess** what happened!" said Kim. "I'm not **fooling**. I just had the best meal on Mars."

Comprehension

Genre

A **Fantasy** is a made-up story that could not really happen.

Reread

Make Predictions

As you read, use your **Predictions Chart**.

What I Predict	What Happens

Read to Find Out

Where are Blue Jay and Elephant going?

200

Blue Jay Finds a Way

by Fran Manushkin

illustrated by Barry Rockwell

201

Blue Jay wanted to fly to the moon.

"Here I go!" said Blue Jay.

He flapped his wings
and flew and flew.

But he did not reach the moon.

It was too far.

Blue Jay told his friend Elephant,

"I want to go to the moon,

but I cannot find a way.

I am feeling sad.

I am a blue Blue Jay."

"I can help you find a way,"
said Elephant.

"You can?" asked Blue Jay.

"I can!" said Elephant.

"I'll take you to the moon. Hop on!"
Elephant began to run.

She flapped her ears like wings.

She ran to the end of the cliff and jumped.

But she did not reach the moon.

She rolled down the hill,

down, down, down.

She made Blue Jay a slide.

"Whee!" shouted Blue Jay.

"That was fun," laughed Blue Jay.

"But I still want to find a way
to the moon!"

"I can help you find a way," said Elephant.

"You can?" asked Blue Jay.

"I can!" said Elephant. "Let's go on this boat.
Hop on!"

Elephant rowed the boat with her trunk.

She rowed and rowed.

But the boat just went around and around.

Then it tipped right over.

SPLASH!

Elephant fell out of the boat!

She sank into the mud.

Blue Jay got a cold shower.

"That was fun!" laughed Blue Jay.

"But I still want to find a way to the moon!"

"We won't give up," said Elephant.

"Let's ride this bike into **space**. Hop on!"

Blue Jay put on a small **helmet**.

Elephant put on a HUGE one.

Elephant began to pedal.

They rode through the woods.

They passed squirrels and **birds** and a skunk.

They even saw a **bear**.

"Look!" shouted Elephant. "We are in the stars!"

Blue Jay said, "Those are not stars.

They are fireflies!"

"I know what we can do," said Elephant.

"One, two, three…" she counted.

"What are you doing?" asked Blue Jay.

"Can you **guess**?" asked Elephant.

"You are counting fireflies!" said Blue Jay.

"Can I help?"

"You can!" said Elephant.

Elephant pointed with her trunk.

And Blue Jay counted.

"Four, five, six, seven."

"Elephant," said Blue Jay,

"I am having such a good time with you.

Let's stay right here on **Earth**."

"It's getting late," said Elephant.

"I'm hungry," said Blue Jay.

"Dinner is waiting on our **table**,"
said Elephant.

"Let's go!" said Blue Jay.

"I'll take you. Hop on!" said Elephant.

"Look!" Blue Jay shouted.

"We are at the moon! No **fooling**!"

"I see it," cried Elephant.

"It is right here in this puddle!"

"I did find a way to the moon!" laughed Blue Jay.

"You did," said Elephant.

"Watch me fly over the moon!" called Blue Jay.

"Watch me jump over it!" shouted Elephant.

Blue Jay and Elephant
followed the moon
from puddle
to puddle,
jumping and flying
all the way home.

Meet Fran Manushkin

Fran Manushkin loved to read as a child. As an adult she loves studying animals and often takes a lot of pictures of them. Recently she's been watching elephants on the Internet. This inspired her to write *Blue Jay Finds a Way*.

Other books by Fran Manushkin

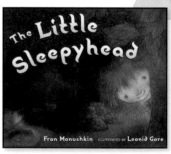

LOG ON Find out more about Fran Manushkin at **www.macmillanmh.com**

Author's Purpose

Fran Manushkin wanted to write about an animal adventure. Write a story about two animals having an adventure.

Comprehension Check

Retell the Story

Use the Retelling Cards to retell the story in order.

Retelling Cards

Think and Compare

What I Predict	What Happens

1. Did you predict Blue Jay would go to the moon? What really happened?

2. Have you ever pretended you were in a very different place? What was it like?

3. How are Blue Jay and Elephant like real people?

4. What do Blue Jay and Kim in "A Good Trip into Space" both like to do?

Meet Ellen Ochoa

Ellen Ochoa was the first Hispanic woman **astronaut.** She has made many trips into space. Ellen lives in Houston, Texas.

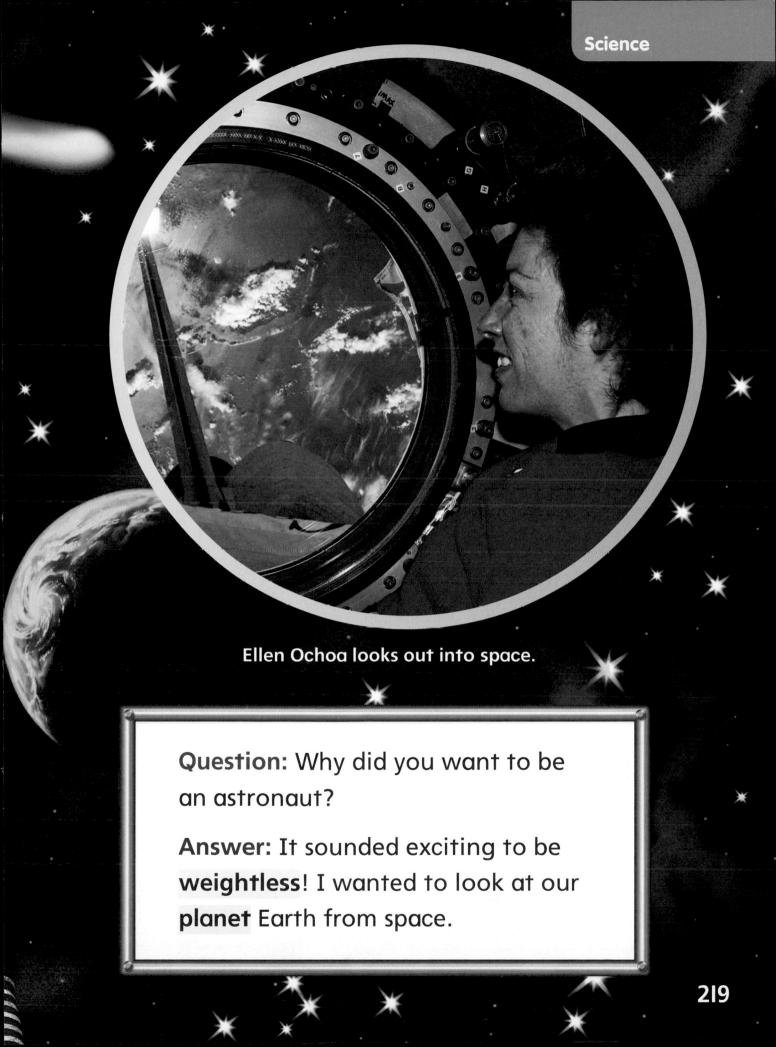

Ellen Ochoa looks out into space.

Question: Why did you want to be an astronaut?

Answer: It sounded exciting to be **weightless**! I wanted to look at our **planet** Earth from space.

Question: What should kids who want to be astronauts do?

Answer: They should study math and science and go to college. They should like learning new things and working in a team.

Ellen Ochoa with her team before going into space

Ellen Ochoa inside a space module

Question: What's it like to be in space?

Answer: It's a lot of fun! You're floating and so is everything else! It's easy to move heavy things. It's easy to reach things, too.

Lunch in Space

- Peanut butter or chicken salad in a tortilla
- Space s'mores (marshmallows and chocolate bar in a tortilla)
- Water or apple juice

SPACE FOOD

FREEZE-DRIED STRAWBERRIES

FRAISES
LYOPHILISÉES

GEFRIESGETROCKNETE
ERDBEEREN

BEVRIESDROGIGE
AARDBEIEN

8g ℮

BEST BEFORE:

★ MADE IN THE U.S.A. ★

Question: How was the food in space?

Answer: The food was very good. We took freeze-dried food and powdered drinks with us. We added hot or cold water. We ate a lot of tortillas. It's easy to put stuff in them.

Tea w/Lemon
& Artificial Sweetener

Lemon-Lime Drink

Question: What's the hardest thing about your job?

Answer: You have to learn a lot. And make sure you learn it before you leave Earth!

Ellen Ochoa works at the space station.

Connect and Compare

What might Blue Jay ask Ellen Ochoa?

Predicates

The **predicate** of a sentence tells what the subject does or is.

Write About Pretending

Anna wrote about pretending to be an astronaut.

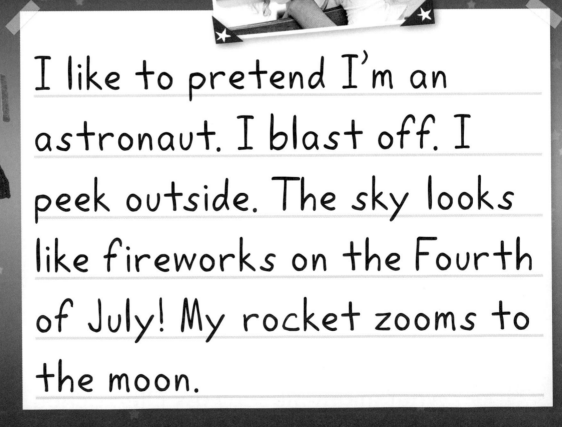

I like to pretend I'm an astronaut. I blast off. I peek outside. The sky looks like fireworks on the Fourth of July! My rocket zooms to the moon.

Your Turn

Think about something you like to pretend to be.

Write about it.

Tell what you do and imagine.

Writer's Checklist

☑ Will readers understand my story?

☑ Does each sentence have a **predicate**?

☑ Do special names like holidays begin with a capital letter?

Talk About It

What jobs do you know about? What jobs would you like to do?

 Find out more about jobs at
www.macmillanmh.com

At Work

Words to Know

ever

interesting

only

laugh

goes

ordinary

---

tools

moon

Do you **ever** think about what you want to be? You could find an **interesting** job. You **only** need to think about what you like!

Do you like to help people? You could be a doctor or a teacher. Do you like to make people **laugh**? You could be a clown or an actor. Do you like to work with tools? You could make houses or fix cars.

You could work at home. Or you could be someone who **goes** to the moon. You could like a job that seems **ordinary**, or one that does not. Think about what you like to do. Then you can find your best job!

Cool Jobs

What would it be like to have these three jobs?

Zoo Dentist

If you were a zoo dentist, you could fix and clean a tiger's teeth. You could fill a hole in an alligator's tooth. You might even pull out an elephant's tusk!

Zoo dentists fix teeth like **ordinary** dentists do. But they work on wild animals who might bite! So the dentist gives the animal medicine. Then it **goes** to sleep. Now the dentist can go to work.

Zoo dentists use big drills to clean out holes in teeth. Big metal tools can help them grip a bad tooth and pull it out. If it's a lion tooth, that can be a pretty big job!

Flavor Maker

Did you **ever** want to change the taste of a food? If you were a flavor maker, you could! You could make medicine taste like cherry or pizza. With **only** a few drops, you could make a hot dog taste like a banana.

Flavor makers work in a lab. They use chemicals to make flavors. Their best tools are their noses and mouths. They do a lot of tasting and smelling!

Flavor makers help make a lot of tasty food! Can you think of a new flavor for a food that you like?

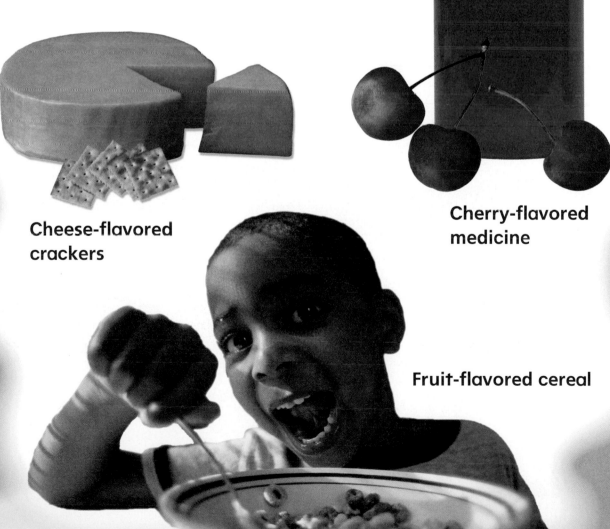

Cheese-flavored crackers

Cherry-flavored medicine

Fruit-flavored cereal

233

Beekeeper

Bees make honey. A beekeeper helps the bees do their job.

If you were a beekeeper, you would build hives for bees to live in. These are not like the hives bees make themselves. Beekeepers make hives out of wood.

How do beekeepers get the honey with all of those stinging bees? They have special clothes to keep the bees from stinging them. There are gloves and a hood. There is a net that goes over the beekeeper's face.

Sometimes beekeepers put smoke into the hives. That makes the bees fly away. Then the beekeepers can take the honey out. It can take a lot of work to get honey. But the end is always sweet!

There are many **interesting** jobs in the world. This person's job is to dress up like a giant bird at sports events. It's fun to make people **laugh**.

What kinds of cool jobs can you think of? What cool job would you like to have?

Comprehension Check

Tell What You Learned

What different kinds of jobs did you learn about?

Think and Compare

1. Which jobs in "Cool Jobs" are about making things? Which jobs are about helping?

2. Which job in "Cool Jobs" was most interesting to you? Why?

3. What makes a job a good job?

4. How are the jobs in "A Job for You" like the jobs in "Cool Jobs"? How are they different?

Jobs at School

Do you want to work at a school? You could be a teacher. But there are lots of other jobs you could do at school, too.

You could be a school nurse. You would take care of sick kids. You would bandage cuts and scrapes.

Do you like to fix things? You could be a custodian. You would keep things clean. You would make sure that everything is working.

Do you like to cook? You could work in the lunchroom. You would make sure the kids at school have good food to eat.

There are lots of fun jobs at school. But the best part is being with so many kids!

Go On ▶

Directions: Answer the questions.

1. What is this story MAINLY about?

  ○ kids going to school

  ○ eating good foods

  ○ working in a school

Tip
Think about what you know.

2. Who can help you if your chair breaks?

  ○   ○   ○

3. You know from reading this story that

  ○ many people work in schools.

  ○ only teachers work in schools.

  ○ nurses help cook good foods.

Write About an Interesting Job

Edgar wrote about a job that he thinks is interesting. He made sure his sentences were clear.

Driving a bulldozer is a very good job. Bulldozers help make roads and buildings. They are very strong. Driving a bulldozer is fun. You push dirt and rocks around. You even get to push down buildings.

240

Your Writing Prompt

Write a report about a job that you are interested in. Tell why you are interested in that job. Make sure your sentences are clear and organized.

Writer's Checklist

☑ Does my report include details about the job?

☑ Did I make my sentences clear?

☑ Did I check my writing for mistakes?

Talk About It

How do baby animals change as they grow up?

LOG ON Find out more about growing animals at **www.macmillanmh.com**

Watching Animals Grow

Words to Know

cub

eyes

learn

enough

air

wild

across

———————

p<u>aw</u>s

j<u>aw</u>s

Read to Find Out

How do bear cubs change as they get older?

A Bear Cub

When a bear **cub** is born, its **eyes** are closed. But it does not need to see to eat. The tiny bear cub drinks milk. He does not need to **learn** how because he just knows how. After a while, he is strong **enough** to go out into the fresh **air**.

Then, it is time to go out into the **wild** where he will learn to hunt. He will be grown-up soon. He will wade **across** streams to catch fish. His strong paws and jaws will help him eat the meat. He will also eat berries from plants.

245

Comprehension

Genre
Nonfiction gives information about a topic.

Summarize
Compare and Contrast
As you read, use your **Compare and Contrast Chart.**

Cub	Grown-up
1	1
2	2
3	3

Read to Find Out
How is a tiger cub different from a grown-up tiger?

246

A Tiger Cub Grows Up

by Joan Hewett

photographs by
Richard Hewett

In the Nursery

Tara is a tiger **cub**.

She was born in a **wild** animal park.

The cub is hungry.

She feels the tip of the bottle.

She drinks her warm milk.

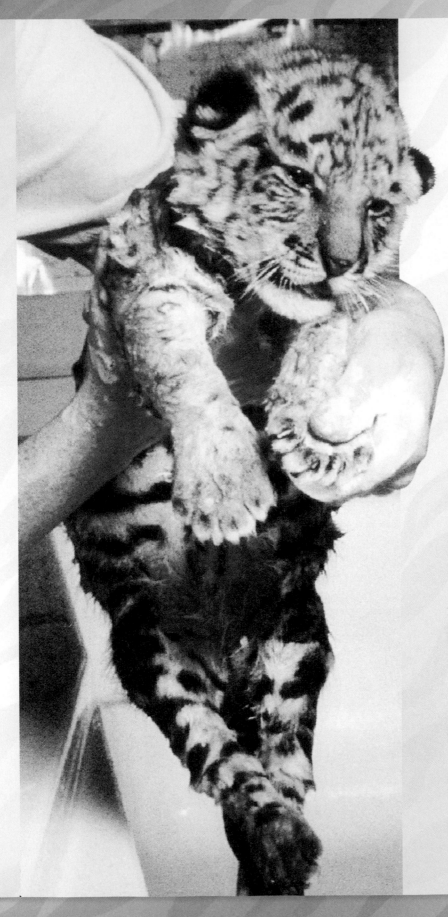

When Tara is
9 days old,
her **eyes** open.

Grown-up tigers like to swim. But little Tara does not like her first bath.

Mary feeds Tara.
She talks to the tiger cub.
She gives her kisses.

At night, Mary takes the cub home with her.
Tara drinks her milk.
She falls asleep.

Then Tara wakes up.
She is hungry!
She wants more milk.

Tara drinks until her belly is full.
She falls back to sleep.
As she sleeps, she grunts
and squeals.

Tara is 3 weeks old.
Her baby teeth are coming in.
She has pointed teeth for tearing meat.

And she has rounded teeth for chewing.

Chewing feels good. But a plastic tray
is hard to hold with chubby paws.

Each day, Mary shows the cub a piece of meat.
Tara does not want to try it. Not yet!

Playtime is a time to **learn**.
Can Tara crawl over Mary's legs?
How hard will Mary let her bite?

Tara is 3 months old. Mary takes Tara to the animal doctor. It is time for a checkup.

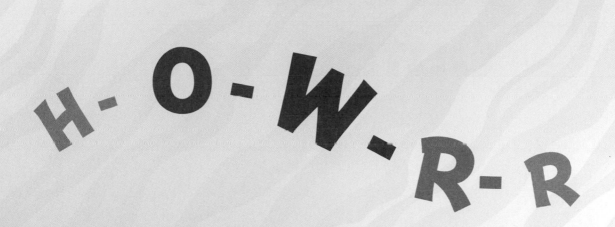

The bright lights are scary. The tiger cub roars.

H-O-W-R-R

Tara Goes Outdoors

Tara is healthy. And she is old **enough** to play outside.

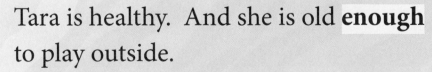

Grass and sky seem strange to Tara.
The **air** is filled with new smells.
The tiger cub follows her nose.
She runs **across** the grass.

Lynn takes care of Tara now.
Lynn hugs Tara. She plays with Tara.
She shows her falling leaves.

Lynn plays with Tara every day.
She teaches Tara what she can do.
She teaches Tara what she cannot do.

Tara greets Lynn with a friendly chuffing sound.
Lynn returns the greeting.

Climbing over Lynn is fun.
Following Lynn is fun.
Tara creeps along the ground.
Then she pounces!

Tara Joins the Grown-up Tigers

Tara is 9 months old. She is big and strong. She can join the park's grown-up Tigers. Tara likes her new home. She can run across the grass. She can climb on logs. She can nap under leafy trees.

Tara watches the big tigers swim.
She walks around the pond. It is hot.
So Tara jumps in. Tara is 1 year old.
The tiger cub has grown up.

S·P·L·A·S·H

Watching Animals with the Hewetts

Joan Hewett thinks research is the most difficult, interesting, and fun part of writing. Many of her books are about baby animals living in zoos or rescue centers.

Richard Hewett says, "I think children's books are the best." He often photographs pictures for books written by his wife, Joan Hewett.

Other books by the Hewetts

LOG ON Find out more about Joan Hewett and Richard Hewett at **www.macmillanmh.com**

Author's Purpose

Joan Hewett wanted to give information about a baby animal. Write about a baby animal you know. Tell how it changed as it grew.

Comprehension Check

Retell the Story

Use the Retelling Cards to retell the story.

Retelling Cards

Think and Compare

Cub	Grown-up
1	1
2	2
3	3

1. What is Tara like at three months old? What is she like at nine months old?

2. What was the most interesting thing you learned about tigers?

3. Can a one-year-old child take care of itself like a one-year-old tiger? Why or why not?

4. How are Tara and the cub in "A Bear Cub" alike?

Poetry

Genre
A **Poem** uses words that sound good together.

 Literary Element
Poets often use words in fun and interesting ways. This is called **Word Play**.

 Find out more about growing animals at **www.macmillanmh.com**

The Tiger

by
Douglas Florian

I am a cat – come hear me purrrr.
I've many stripes upon my furrrr.
I speed through forests like a blurrrr.
I hunt at night – I am tigerrrr.

Connect and Compare

How is the tiger in this poem different from the tiger in *A Tiger Cub Grows Up*?

Writing

Pronouns

Use *I* in the subject of a sentence.
Use *me* in the predicate.

Write About a Vet

Chris wrote a report about a vet.

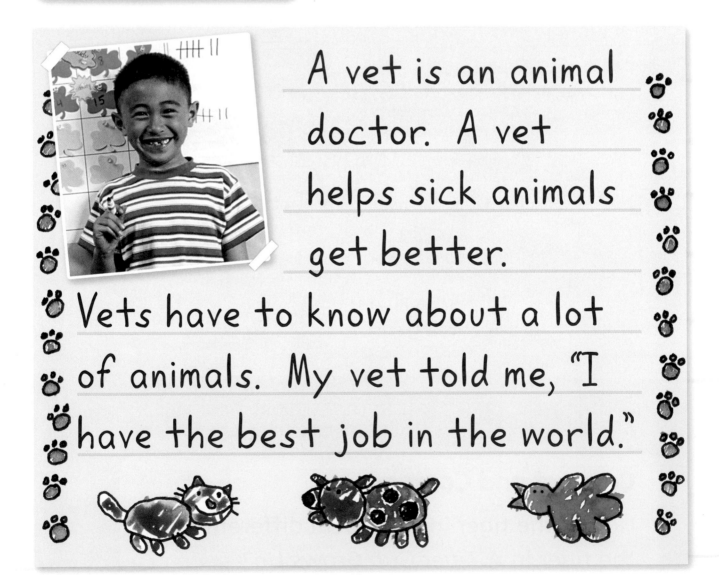

A vet is an animal doctor. A vet helps sick animals get better.

Vets have to know about a lot of animals. My vet told me, "I have the best job in the world."

Your Turn

What does a vet do?

Find out some facts.

Write a report.

Writer's Checklist

☑ Did my report have facts?

☑ Did I use the pronouns *I* and *me* correctly?

☑ Did I use a capital letter for the pronoun *I*?

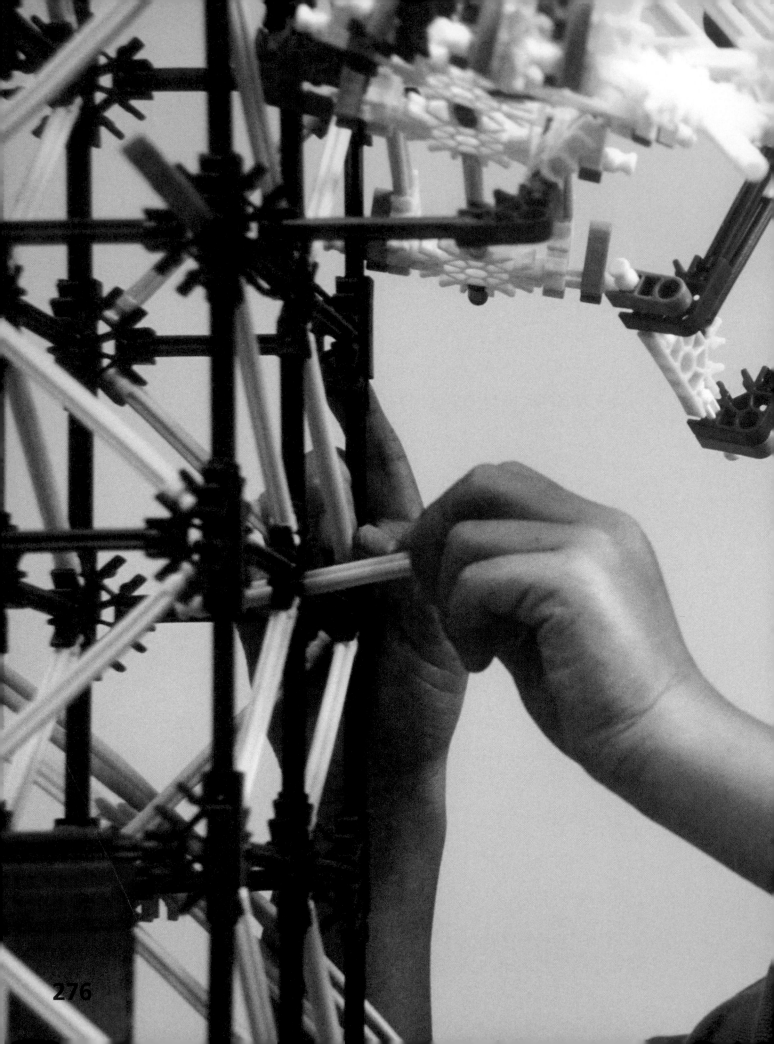

Talk About It

What kind of playhouse would you like? How would you build it?

LOG ON Find out more about building at
www.macmillanmh.com

Let's Build

Words to Know

circle

toward

leave

grew

toppled

wreck

welcoming

_____

Joy

join

Read to Find Out

How does the town grow?

The Town that Grew

Joy and Ron were making a town. Joy made a **circle** of shops. She put the houses **toward** one end of town. Ron added a school. "Let's not **leave** out a bike path," said Joy.

The town **grew** quickly. But then, Joy's dog ran into town. The houses **toppled**.

"Max, you can join us," said Joy. "Just don't **wreck** our town."

The kids fixed things up. Then they added a flag **welcoming** one and all to their joyful town.

Comprehension

Genre
Realistic Fiction is a made-up story that could really happen.

Summarize

STRATEGY SKILL

Cause and Effect
As you read, use your **Cause and Effect Chart**.

Cause → Effect

Read to Find Out
What will the children do to build a sand castle?

280

Sand Castle

by Brenda Shannon Yee
illustrated by Thea Kliros

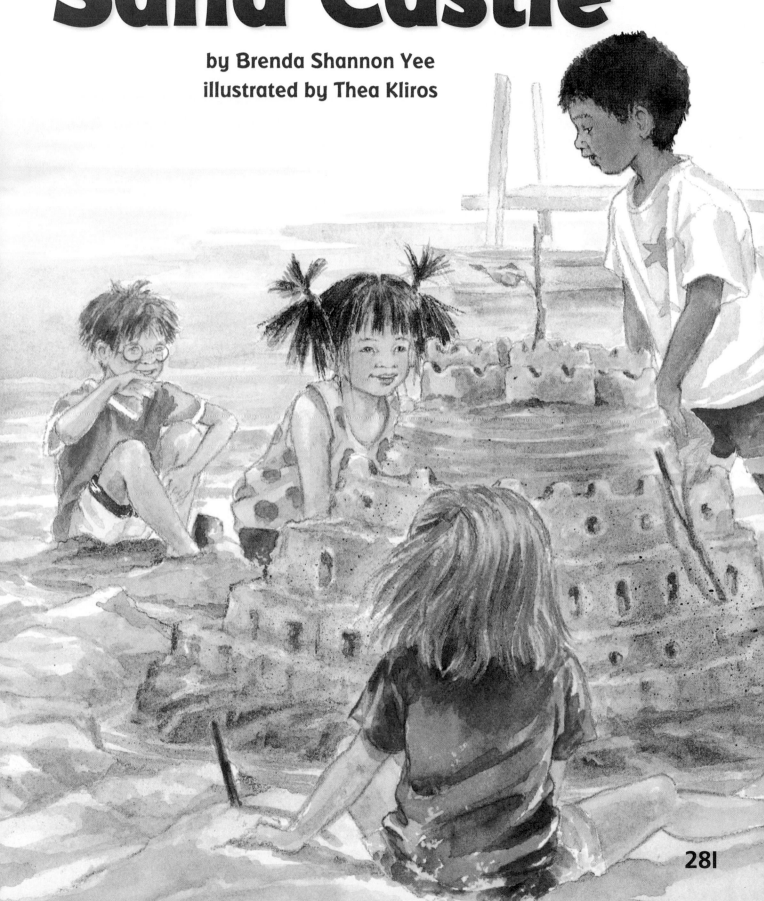

Jen dug the sand with her shovel.
A boy with a bucket watched.
"Can I help?" he asked.
"I am building a sand castle," said Jen.

"Your castle needs a moat," said the boy.
He dug a **circle** around Jen's castle with
his bucket.

The castle **grew** taller.
The moat grew deeper.

"Can I help?" asked a girl with a spoon.
"I am making the moat," said the boy.
"This is my castle," said Jen.

"If I dig a path to the lake, the moat will fill up with water," the girl said.

She scooped a path in the sand.
Water sloshed into the path and
headed **toward** the moat.

The castle grew taller.
The moat grew deeper.
The path grew wider.

"Can I help?" asked a boy with a cup.
"I am digging the path to the water,"
   said the girl.

"I am making the moat," said the boy.

"This is my castle," said Jen.

"You will need a wall to protect your castle,"
said the boy with the cup.

The boy filled the cup with wet sand.
Pat, pat. He turned it over.
Tap, tap. One sand block stood.
Pat, tap. Two sand blocks.

The castle grew taller.
The moat grew deeper.
The path grew wider.
The wall grew longer.

"Can I help?" asked a girl holding a rake.

"I am building the wall," said the boy with the cup.
"I am digging the path to the water," said the girl with the spoon.
"I am making the moat," said the boy with the bucket.

"This is my castle," said Jen.

"You need a road, so people can get to the castle," said the girl with the rake.

Dragging the rake in the sand, the girl traced a winding road. With the rake teeth, she swirled wavy shapes.

Hands patted and pushed the squishy sand.

The castle rose high.

The moat dipped deep.

The path flowed long.

The wall stood strong.

The road lay wide and **welcoming**.

Shadows stretched across the sand.

"Angela! Time to go!"

"Robert! We're leaving!"

"Tanisha! It's late!"

"Louis! Rinse your feet!"

"Jen! Say good–bye!"

"But what about the castle?
We worked so hard," Tanisha said.

"As soon as we **leave**, someone
will **wreck** it," said Louis.

"I know what to do!" Jen said.
Splat! She jumped on the castle.

In a flurry they all kicked the road, **toppled** the wall, flattened the path, filled the moat, and crushed the castle.

"Good–bye!" the beach friends shouted as they scattered across the cooling sand. "Let's do it again tomorrow!"

Meet the Author and Illustrator

Brenda Shannon Yee says she got the idea for this story while building a sand castle with her children at the beach.

Thea Kliros says, "As a child, I was read to every night." She hopes her illustrations will help children enjoy and love books.

Another book by Brenda Shannon Yee

Another book by Thea Kliros

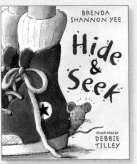

LOG ON Find out more about Brenda Shannon Yee and Thea Kliros at **www.macmillanmh.com**

Author's Purpose

Brenda Shannon Yee wanted to tell a story about building a sand castle. Write about something you can build. Tell how you would build it.

Comprehension Check

Retell the Story

Use the Retelling Cards to retell the story.

Retelling Cards

Think and Compare

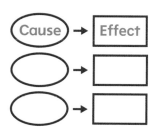

1. What happens when the other kids help Jen build?

2. What do you like to do in the sand or at the beach?

3. Why do children sometimes wreck a sand castle they made?

4. How are *Sand Castle* and "The Town that Grew" alike? How are they different?

Build with Sand and Ice

Lots of people **build** with bricks and stones. But some build with sand and ice. How do they make these great **structures**?

Builders dig a deep hole and scoop out the wet sand to make a castle like this. Next, they make the wet sand into pancakes. They stack the pancakes to make towers.

Then, its time to carve the sand! Knives and spoons are good tools for making windows, doors, and steps.

This ice castle in Minnesota was built for a winter festival.

Take a look at this castle! It's made of ice. People use saws to cut blocks of ice from a **frozen** lake. A crane piles up the blocks. The castle gets higher and higher. Some ice castles are 20 stories tall!

In the Ice Hotel in Sweden, everything is made of ice.

In this hotel, the floors, walls, and beds are ice! Sleeping bags keep visitors warm when they sleep. The Ice Hotel melts every spring. So a new one must be built every year!

Connect and Compare

How are the castles in this story like the one the children made in *Sand Castle*?

Combining Sentences

You can use the word *and* to **combine sentences** that have the same subject.

Write a Story

Isabel wrote a story about making a clubhouse.

One day Erin and Devi found a huge cardboard box. "Let's make a clubhouse," said Erin. They painted it and made a sign. It said, "Best Friends' Club."

Your Turn

Two friends find a huge cardboard box.

What could they do with it?

Write about it.

Writer's Checklist

☑ Did I indent the first sentence?

☑ Did I use *and* to combine sentences that have the same subject?

☑ Did the special names begin with capital letters?

Test Strategy

Author and Me
Think about what
the author tells you.
Think about what
you know.

First a Caterpillar... Then a Butterfly

The little caterpillar doesn't seem like much. It hatches from a tiny egg and creeps and eats and creeps and eats. When it gets fat, the little caterpillar makes some changes.

The caterpillar makes itself a hard shell or case. It hangs upside down. Inside, the caterpillar changes. Now it is called a pupa.

Go on ▶

In about ten days, it comes out. Now it is a butterfly. The butterfly tests its wings. Soon it is ready to fly away and begin a new life.

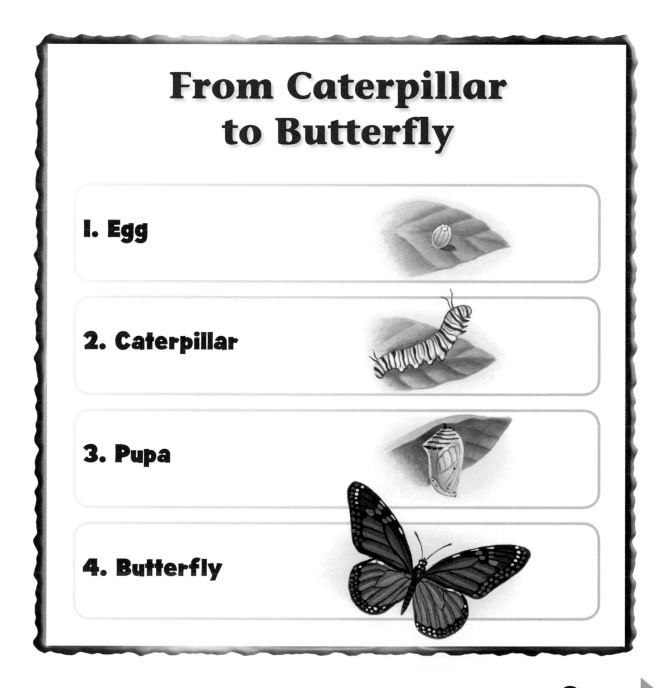

From Caterpillar to Butterfly

1. Egg

2. Caterpillar

3. Pupa

4. Butterfly

Go on ▶ 313

Tip

Think about what you know.

**Directions:
Answer the questions.**

I. Which picture shows something that a caterpillar CANNOT do?

◯   ◯   ◯

2. What happens to the caterpillar inside the shell?

◯ It turns into a spider.

◯ It turns into a butterfly.

◯ It turns into an egg.

3. How does the hard shell help the caterpillar?

◯ It looks pretty.

◯ It holds the caterpillar's eggs.

◯ It protects the caterpillar.

Go on ▶

Writing Prompt

Did you ever see an interesting insect?
Write about it. What did it look like?
What did it do? Write four or
more sentences.

Glossary

What is a Glossary?

A glossary can help you to find the meanings of words. The words are listed in alphabetical order. You can look up a word and read it in a sentence. Sometimes there is a picture.

Sample Entry

Letter

C c

children — Main Entry

This ride is only for **children**.

Sentence

Aa

across

Mike walked **across** the bridge.

air

In the garden, the **air** smelled like flowers.

along

The boys hiked **along** a river.

always

Paul **always** arrives late.

animal

An elephant
is a big **animal**.

artists

Artists are showing their paintings in the gym.

astronaut

An **astronaut** may travel to the moon.

athlete

The **athlete** was practicing for the big game.

Bb

ball

Alex hit the **ball** as far as she could.

bear

A **bear** likes to eat berries.

beautiful

Mary's painting is **beautiful**.

been

The boys were dirty because they had **been** playing in the mud.

319

better

Greg likes apples **better** than pears.

bird

The **bird** sits on a branch.

build

We used bricks to **build** the house.

Cc

children

This ride is only for **children**.

circle

Draw a **circle** to make the snowman's head.

clues

The **clues** helped Jim solve the mystery.

color

My favorite **color** is yellow because it looks like the sun.

crowded

This playground is always **crowded** with kids.

cub

A lion **cub** stays near its mother.

Dd

disabilities

Her **disabilities** didn't stop Miko from trying anything.

discovery

The scientist hopes to make a great **discovery**.

discs

The **discs** we threw flew through the air.

Ee

early

Pete wakes us **early** in the morning.

earth

The **earth** has many oceans and lakes.

enough

There was **enough** pizza for everyone.

errand

Tom ran an **errand** for his mom.

ever

Do not **ever** swim alone!

eyes

This cat has yellow **eyes**.

Ff

father

Jack and his **father** are cooking dinner.

firm

The teacher is **firm** about the rules.

fooling

I was **fooling** when I said I had a pet lion.

from

I got a letter **from** my friend.

frozen

It was so cold that the lake had **frozen**.

Gg

glide

A toy plane can **glide** on air.

goes

A train **goes** fast.

gone

The pickles are all **gone**.

grew

The little plant **grew**.

ground

Joe dug a hole in the **ground**.

guess

I took a **guess** about what was in the box.

Hh

head

I bumped my **head**.

helmet

Keisha wears a **helmet** when she rides her bike.

Ii

insects

All **insects** have six legs and three body parts.

instead

I chose the red shirt **instead** of the blue one.

interesting

I read an **interesting** book!

invisible

The brown lizard is almost **invisible** on the sand.

Ll

laugh

My friends tell jokes that make me **laugh**.

laughter

There is a lot of **laughter** when we all play together.

learn

I **learn** to play the piano.

leave

Children **leave** the school at 3 o'clock.

love

I **love** my pet.

Mm

machine

A **machine** can help sew clothes.

meadow

The **meadow** is full of flowers.

mother

My **mother** always braids my hair.

motors

Motors helped the boats go faster.

Nn

never

I **never** go to sleep without a story.

nothing

I bought **nothing** at the store.

nursery

The new babies are in the **nursery**.

Oo

only

There was **only** one pencil left.

or

Do you want the big doll **or** the small one?

ordinary

On an **ordinary** day, Pam plays outside after school.

other

Sarah ran and the **other** kids walked.

Pp

part

Alex shared **part** of his sandwich.

perhaps

Perhaps the sun will come out later.

place

The beach is a fun **place**!

planet

Saturn is a **planet** with rings.

protects

A helmet **protects** your head when you are on your bike.

Rr

records

Lenny broke all the school's **records** for attendance.

round

A wheel is **round**.

Ss

searching

We are **searching** for bugs in the woods.

sculpture

The artist used clay to make a **sculpture**.

senses

You use your five **senses** to taste, smell, see, hear, and touch.

should

You **should** eat a good lunch.

shout

I **shout** when I'm happy!

space

Rockets go into **space**.

structures

We made some funny **structures** from sticks.

suddenly

Suddenly the room got dark.

supposed

I am **supposed** to go to bed early.

Tt

table

We eat together at the **table**.

thought

He **thought** hard when he took the test.

tiny

A kitten is **tiny**.

toppled

The blocks **toppled** over.

toward

He ran **toward** the store.

try

Kids **try** hard to climb the rope.

Ww

weightless

It would be fun to be **weightless** for a day.

welcoming

She opened the door with a **welcoming** smile.

wild

A **wild** animal finds its own food.

wreck

This old car is a **wreck**.

Acknowledgments

The publisher gratefully acknowledges permission to reprint the following copyrighted material:

Dot & Jabber and the Big Bug Mystery by Ellen Stoll Walsh. Text and illustrations copyright © 2003 by Ellen Stoll Walsh. Reprinted by permission of Harcourt, Inc.

"Flowers at Night" by Aileen Fisher from *The Earth Is Painted Green: A Garden of Poems about Our Planet* by Barbara Brenner, S.D. Schindler, S.D. Curry © 2000, Scholastic. Reprinted with permission of Scholastic Inc.

A Fruit Is a Suitcase for Seeds by Jean Richards, illustrations by Anca Hariton. Text copyright © 2002 by Jean Richards. Illustrations copyright © 2002 by Anca Hariton. Reprinted by permission of The Millbrook Press, Inc.

"The Kite" from *Days with Frog and Toad* by Arnold Lobel. Text and illustrations copyright © 1979 by Arnold Lobel. Reprinted by permission of Harper & Row Publishers, Inc.

Olivia by Ian Falconer. Copyright © 2000 by Ian Falconer. Reprinted by permission of Atheneum Books for Young Readers, an imprint of Simon & Schuster Children's Publishing Division.

Sand Castle by Brenda Shannon Yee, illustrated by Thea Kliros. Text copyright © 1999 by Brenda Shannon Yee. Illustrations copyright © 1999 by Thea Kliros. Reprinted by permission of Greenwillow Books, a division of William Morrow & Company, Inc.

A Tiger Cub Grows Up by Joan Hewett, photographed by Richard Hewett. Text copyright © 2002 by Joan Hewett. Photographs copyright © 2002 by Richard Hewett. Reprinted by permission of Carolrhoda Books, Inc., a division of Lerner Publishing Group.

"The Tiger" by Douglas Florian from *Mammalabilia: Poems and Paintings* by Douglas Florian. Copyright © 2000 by Douglas Florian. Reprinted with permission of Harcourt Children's Books.

Whistle for Willie by Ezra Jack Keats. Text and illustrations copyright © 1964 by Ezra Jack Keats. Reprinted by permission of the Penguin Group, a division of Penguin Putnam books for Young Readers.

Book Cover, FROG AND TOAD ARE FRIENDS by Arnold Lobel. Copyright © 1970 by Arnold Lobel. Reprinted by permission of HarperCollins Publishers.

Book Cover, GOGGLES! by Ezra Jack Keats. Copyright © 1969 by Ezra Jack Keats. Reprinted by permission of Viking, an imprint of Penguin Putnam Books for Young Readers.

Book Cover, A HARBOR SEAL PUP GROWS UP by Joan Hewett, photographs by Richard Hewett. Text copyright © 2001 by Joan Hewett. Photographs copyright © 2001 by Richard Hewett. Reprinted by permission of Carolrhoda Books, Inc., a division of Lerner Publishing Group.

Book Cover, HIDE & SEEK by Brenda Shannon Yee, illustrated by Debbie Tilley. Text copyright © 2001 by Brenda Shannon Yee. Illustrations copyright © 2001 by Debbie Tilley. Reprinted by permission of Orchard Books, an imprint of Scholastic Inc.

Book Cover, HOP JUMP by Ellen Stoll Walsh. Copyright © 1993 by Ellen Stoll Walsh. Reprinted by permission of Harcourt Brace & Company.

Book Cover, MOUSE PAINT by Ellen Stoll Walsh. Copyright © 1989 by Ellen Stoll Walsh. Reprinted by permission of Harcourt Brace & Company.

Book Cover, OLIVIA AND THE MISSING TOY by Ian Falconer. Copyright © 2003 by Ian Falconer. Reprinted by permission of Atheneum Books for Young Readers, an imprint of Simon & Schuster Children's Publishing Division.

Book Cover, OLIVIA SAVES THE CIRCUS by Ian Falconer. Copyright © 2001 by Ian Falconer. Reprinted by permission of Atheneum Books for Young Readers, an imprint of Simon & Schuster Children's Publishing Division.

Book Cover, OWL AT HOME by Arnold Lobel. Copyright © 1975 by Arnold Lobel. Reprinted by permission of HarperCollins Children's Books, a division of HarperCollins Publishers.

Book Cover, A PENGUIN CHICK GROWS UP by Joan Hewett, photographs by Richard Hewett. Text copyright © 2004 by Joan Hewett. Photographs copyright © 2004 by Richard Hewett. Reprinted by permission of Carolrhoda Books, Inc., a division of Lerner Publishing Group.

Book Cover, THE LITTLE SLEEPYHEAD by Fran Manushkin, illustrated by Leonid Gore. Copyright © 2004 by Fran Manushkin. Reprinted by permission of Dutton Children's Books, a division of Penguin Young Readers Group.

Book Cover, THE SHIVERS IN THE FRIDGE by Fran Manushkin, illustrated by Paul O. Zelinsky. Copyright © 2006 by Fran Manushkin. Reprinted by permission of Dutton Children's Books, a division of Penguin Young Readers Group.

ILLUSTRATION
Cover Illustration: Leland Klanderman

10-11: Tiphanie Beeke. 12-37: Ian Falconer. 38: Nancy Davis. 40: Nancy Davis. 46-47: Jamie Smith. 48-63: Arnold Lobel. 88-89: Michael-Che Swisher. 90-119: Ezra Jack Keats. 132-149: Anca Hariton. 150-151: Lori Lohsteeter. 157: Diane Paterson. 160-161: Will Terry. 162-189: Ellen Stoll Walsh. 190-193: Susan Swan. 198-199: Eileen Hine. 200-217: Barry Rockwell. 218-223: John Kaufmann. 245: Tom Leonard. 272-273: Tom Leonard. 278-279: Sally Vitskey. 280-305: Thea Kilros. 313-315: Tom Leonard. 316-317: Judith Moffatt.

PHOTOGRAPHY
All Photographs are by Macmillan/McGraw Hill (MMH) except as noted below:

8-9: Anthony Bannister/CORBIS. 9: (tr) Annie Reynolds/ PhotoLink/Getty Images, Inc. 36: Roddy McDowell. 38: (b) Ludovic Maisant/CORBIS; (bcr) Pixtal/AGE Fotostock. 39: (t) Malcah Zeldis/Art Resource, NY; (t) C Squared Studios/Getty Images, Inc.;(bcr) Pixtal/AGE Fotostock. 40: (t) Art Resource, NY; (bl) Erich Lessing/Art Resource, NY; (b) Perfect Picture Parts/Alamy; (bcr) Ghislain & Marie David de Lossy The Image Bank/Getty Images, Inc.; (bcr) Pixtal/AGE Fotostock. 41: (t) Victoria & Albert Museum,